Hey! You Never Know...

Witty Vignettes of Life, Adventure and Insight

Lorraine Rose

Manor Publishing Collective

San Diego, CA

LORRAINE ROSE

Lorraine Playing the Piano with a Friend Looking On

∞∞∞

Hey! You Never Know...

Copyright © 2019 by Manor Publishing Collective

All rights reserved.

No part of this book may be reproduced in any form or by any electronic or mechanical means, including information storage and retrieval systems, without written permission from the publisher, except for the use of brief quotations in a book review.

Manor Publishing Collective

Sunny Baker, Publisher

2635 2nd Ave Suite 328

San Diego, CA 92103

admin@manorcollective.com

1st edition
Print on Demand by KDP, an Amazon Company

Kindle Version 1 (with edits and new photos)

Contents

Title Page
Dedication
About the Title, From the Author
The King & I 1
Close-Up 4
Surviving a Divorce 7
Re-Entering Single 9
The First Date 13
Say It with (Silk) Flowers 17
Transportation Trauma 22
The Ultimate Night Out 26
Full House 32
'Tis the Season 36
Another Happy New Year! 40
A Moving Experience 44
Show Place 48
Sprinklers and Saints 52
She Floats Through the Air.... 56
A Male Dummy? 66
From Eel Skin Shoes to Lamb Suede Bikinis 70

Anxiety Attack	74
An Axe Murderer	78
Email, References and Reasons Not to Go--	85
Billy Boy	92
Bobcats and Shoplifting	94
Lorraine Rose:	98
The Manor Publishing Collective	100
Books In This Series	102

Dedication

This book is dedicated to family and friends; it couldn't have been written without you…and to my publisher and editor, Sunny Baker, whose encouragement and skill made it all possible.

About the Title, From the Author

For years "Hey! You Never Know…" has been my stock answer to various (often skeptical) questions:

"Lorraine, you've lived in upstate New York for almost 60 years! Do you think you'll like living all alone in Santa Fe?"

"Lorraine, you aren't Polish and you've never been a teacher! Do you really think you can actually teach English as a second language in Poland?"

"Lorraine, do you REALLY think you'll be happy pulling up stakes and traveling around the United States in a 5th wheel?"

Well, dear reader, one of my favorite quotes is,

"Never be afraid to try something new. Remember, amateurs built the Ark; professionals built the Titanic."
- Louis Menand

Enjoy!

Lorraine Rose, Author

HEY! YOU NEVER KNOW...

The King & I

(A Royal Pain)

Last night my soon-to-be ex-husband dropped in unexpectedly, ostensibly to see the children (who were at a school function), and while there he used the bathroom. He had met with his lawyer that day, and I was to be the recipient of his displeasure. He flew into a rage about money, child custody, ownership of the house, division of furniture...and the lid on the toilet seat! ?????

He was furious because the lid was not down. Not the whole seat, which even used to irritate Dear Abby, but just the lid. I usually put it down, but it really isn't all that offensive when up. The butterfly decals on the underside are rather attractive.

He said when the lid is up, the water evaporates. Complained that he had been putting lids down on toilet seats in our house for 26 years! Then he stormed out of the house.

After he left, I stood there, stunned. Could this have been the major cause of our break-up? I thought of all the books, all those articles, all the psychology I had read trying to find out where I went wrong. (Since he was having an affair, I was sure it was my fault—that something in ME was lacking, or he wouldn't have strayed.) I remembered all those discussions when I tried to reach the seat of the problem...it never occurred to me that it might be a real seat!

Wow, what a breakthrough. Do you realize what this means? Do you have any idea of how many marriages might have been saved had this been discovered sooner? Women's magazines, which I read religiously for years, never featured this one. I mean, I have read about the bourbon-bibbing bride, the sex-starved spouse, the menopausal mama, but this—this is the real biggie!

How many women out there realize that their husband's love may be evaporating right along with the toilet water? Not to be confused with the toilet water in the pretty bottle on my dressing table, on which I always put the lid. Even I know that evaporates.

Wait—could it be he got the two confused? I know they're both water, both are associated with distinctive odors, and then...there is this evaporation thing.... Naah, the man, after all, is an engineer! He has a Master's Degree. Our friends, family, everyone who knows him had been made aware of how intelligent he is. Nope, he must be referring the water IN the toilet.

Well, this information is too late for me, and for so many others, but maybe I can help those who come after. To the young brides just starting out, to women who THINK their marriages are solid, to all those wives out there just waking up to the fact that their marriages may be faltering, take heed. Wives of America, don't leave the cover up on that toilet seat! Trust me. Even though it may seem unimportant to you, there must be some deep-seated (pardon) psychological reason for men to feel this way. In fact, it's evidently so deep that many of them don't even realize that the water evaporation is that important to them. It probably dates back to a feeling of vulnerability when the water in the castle moat became low and was no longer a protection against enemy attack.

By golly, all that talk about a man's home being his castle is true! And here I thought it was just a cliché. And the toilet…(Oh! it's becoming so clear to me now!) That's why they call it the throne!

This adds a whole new meaning to the concept of toilet training. Ladies, remember the importance of that little seat. To all those wives who want to keep their marriages running smoothly, maybe talking out your problems isn't the best course. If your husbands were able to express their deepest feelings, their message to you would probably be: Put a Lid On It!"

Close-Up

CLOSE-UP

The heavy glass door of the Plaza building closes out the dirt and the noise. Even the sounds of the elevators (six of them...no waiting) are subdued. My high heels make no impression in the rug as I step out. The young woman and I automatically smile at each other as she seats me. Everything is automatic today. She's wearing three earrings. One ear is pierced twice. Her ringed hands are beautifully manicured. I glance at mine, naked, without even the adornment of polish. Instinctively looking away from them to the scene outside, I realize again that the view from here is spectacular.

I look out from the ninth floor across to the other buildings. The sun flashes on the windows, making them as bright and impersonal as traffic lights, and below, the Genesee River mirrors the day. The shrubs, grass and little walkways are well-kept. The bridges on the river invite people to pause as they cross and look at what is reflected there. Everything looks cleaner from here, even the grimy side-streets. One reason the view from up high is so lovely is that I'm too far away to see the dirt.

∞∞∞

I have been here before, when my husband surprised me by taking me to the elegant revolving restaurant for our twenty-fourth wedding anniversary. It was on the top floor of this very same building. We had dined unfashionably early so we could see the sky darken, watching the city lights vie with the stars for our attention. I realize now that a young woman was vying with me for my husband's attention although I didn't want to admit it then.

That was almost a year ago. I'm looking at the same panorama and it is still breath-taking, whether it is seen from the top floor in the evening or the ninth floor in the afternoon. The one big difference is my immediate surroundings.

As I turn from the long view of the city to the close-up of the room inside, reality faces me. It's not a romantic restaurant, but an office. The attractive blue-eyed man across from me is my lawyer, not my husband. We're sitting on opposite sides of a desk instead of a table, and we're discussing -- not the menu -- but my divorce.

I'm close enough now to see the dirt.

Surviving a Divorce

Many people out there never planned on being single, and so were unprepared for it. I know, because I'm one of them. Divorce, separation, death…they're all tough—and sad.

I lost my husband after over 25 years of marriage. Well, he didn't actually DIE, I just lost him. He came down with a case of mid-life crisis, complicated by attacks of infidelity. It wasn't fatal to him, but it sure deep-sixed the marriage.

In retrospect, it might have been easier if he had died. That sounds harsh, I know, but at least I wouldn't have felt like such a failure, or been heartsick wondering what went wrong. I'm still not sure, as far as that goes, but the point is, if he had been taken from me through death it would have been no fault of mine. Well. Unless my fingerprints were actually found on the gun.

My lawyer talked me into at least TRYING divorce first. I reluctantly agreed. What the heck. I could always shoot him later.

People react in various ways to divorce: drinking,

drugs, overeating, homicide, suicide…. Suicide might have become a reality, too, but I simply could not persuade him to do it, no matter how hard I tried. I told him, "Hey, it's a great way to get rid of your guilt." You know, he never was one for trying new things.

These things happen. Sometimes happiness comes out of tragedy. I mean, look at us. He got what HE wanted, she got what SHE wanted. Of course she got what I wanted too. Just couldn't make it come out happy for everyone. But the important thing is how we come out of it, right? No matter whose fault it is? Like they used to say, "It's not whether you win or lose, but how you play the game" (didn't we only hear that when we lost?) and that "Time heals all wounds"?

Hey! Wait a minute! I don't think so! Maybe we're not supposed to flip people off, but we CAN flip some of those old sayings. How about, "It's not whether you win or lose, but how you place the blame!" Yeah! Or how about this one? "Time wounds all heels!" Right!

Hopefully, one's sense of humor returns. You find yourself saying things like, "A funny thing happened to me on my way to our 25th wedding anniversary: I stumbled over a triangle and BOY did I get hurt!"

Abe Lincoln once said, "You're just about as happy as you want to be". Okay, Abe, I'll keep that in mind. I hope you, dear reader, do too.

Re-Entering Single

Would a convent take a divorced mother of five children? Perhaps that seems a little needy. (Needy? NEEDY? How about flippin' DESPERATE??)

Well, those many years ago, that's how I felt. The divorce was over after three long days in court. Emotions were settling like tiny particles in the air after a dust storm. I was single again, after a quarter-of-a-century of marriage. Instinctively I knew that NOW was the time to panic. The eagles in my chest started flapping wildly, giving me an anxiety attack that was the granddaddy of them all. I kept taking deep breaths, reassuring myself, "Hang in there...you're going to be fine...the worst is over...." (Did I really believe that?)

I didn't even know how to act or think as one person, not half of a couple. Well, I could learn, right? I'd heard of support groups for single people. How do others handle it? No more staying at home crying. I was determined to pick myself up by the scruff of the neck and put myself back in the world. I made some calls and went to my first meeting, in which the topic was

"Re-entering Society as a Single Person". Perfect. Or so I thought.

After the orientation, we sat at tables with 3x5 cards and pencils on them. The president of the organization explained that these were for asking questions of a guest counselor. Not too many people were writing. I was temporarily paralyzed from the shoulders down. All I could do was look around, dropping my eyes immediately if anyone looked back.

The counselor, a psychotherapist, gave us her credentials and urged us to ask **anything** we wanted to know. The President said he realized some questions might be rather sensitive (my eyes closed involuntarily) but we needn't give names. Someone would collect the cards and give them to the counselor. Still, not too many were writing. Finally the President said, reassuringly, "Look I know many of you have questions, or you wouldn't be here. No subject is taboo. For instance, a question someone might have is, 'Should you have sex on the first date?'"

This time my eyes widened in sheer shock. I must've let out some kind of strangled sound, because a couple of people at my table looked at me, concerned. The woman next to me put her hand on my arm and asked softly, "Is there something wrong?" I saw through my panic that she was at least 15 years younger than I. I shook my head and smiled weakly. How could I tell her that I was aghast at this question that she and everyone seemed to take so calmly?

Sex on the first date! **The first date??** When I was dating we didn't even **kiss** on the first date! Good heavens, what was I in for? Suddenly I just wanted to go home. I would have, too, but didn't want to call any more attention to myself. I remember little of the discussion because I was mentally wondering what I would do on… <u>The First Date</u>. I sure couldn't go to mom with this one. Assuming a man finally broke through my barriers and was persuasive enough, what would it be like? What would I do? How would I act? Never mind that…dear Lord, how would HE act? And what could I do to **stop** him?

Okay. Besides donning a high-necked, long-sleeved dress (and if it was winter, I'd **really** bundle up), I'd wear my cross **prominently.** For drinks, I'd order either a glass of Blue Nun or a Virgin Mary, to give the evening religious overtones.

When it came to the crucial goodnight at the door, I could accidentally pull out my rosary instead of my keys. **That** ought to do it. (Sure, Lorraine, why don't you go one more and wear a necklace of garlic while you're at it? Is this the first date, or the first bite?)

After the meeting there was dancing. Not for me. As I gathered up my things to leave I noticed a man walking toward my table. Horrified, I realized he was headed for **me**. How nice it was to learn he was the vice-president, doing his job to welcome newcomers. Whew. Okay. Nothing personal. He had a gentle, easy manner which put me at ease and I confided my fool-proof plan for dating, along with my plans for a religious vocation. He laughed with me, but had the perspicacity to see through my "joke-screen".

It's kind of like driving a car," he said of my new single status. "As though you haven't driven for a long time, and suddenly **you** have to do all the driving." He smiled, leaned over and said softly, "You don't have to go any faster, or any farther than you want to."

Right! Who says I have to drive on the expressway during rush hour? Yeah, or plan any long-distance trips? What a relief. The pressure was off. Sure, I was re-entering society as a single person, but there was no fine print that said 'swinging single!' I could drive at my own speed. And maybe keep a rosary in my coat pocket.

The First Date

It's rough on a parent when teenagers start dating but I bet it can't compare to the feelings teenagers must experience when a parent begins dating. Divorce brings this out quickly, especially when it comes to a parent and...THE OPPOSITE SEX. (Listen—did you hear that sinister music just now? It's always heard when the words "parent" and "opposite sex" are in the same sentence.) It probably never occurred to them before that a parent can be as shy, nervous, scared and silly (I was sure scared silly) as any teenager when it comes to socializing.

To my relief, it was quite a while before anyone broke through my reserve and asked me out. The horse-blinders I put on as soon as I left the house may have had something to do with it. My daughter caught me wearing them though, and took them away.

However, if one looks straight ahead, not making eye contact with anyone, it's almost as effective...a tad less obvious, too. It's not that I'm painfully shy or uncomfortable around strangers, but my self-confidence had received a knockout blow and was still shakily trying to recover.

Someone finally did break through and ask me out. An older man, pleasant, introduced by a family member at a wedding reception. Mutual friends had known him for years. Couldn't get much safer than that. He called a few times and finally persuaded me to go out for dinner and dancing. Now. My kids had heard me talking to him on the phone and had taken messages from him, and I'm sure they thought I would go out with him… someday. Probably in about five years or so.

Well. My 16 year old son eyed me warily when I told him that dinner was in the oven and to be sure to leave the kitchen neat. My daughter, 18, made two observations: first, Mom had eye shadow on and next, the table was only set for two. "You're going OUT?" said she. "On a DATE?" asked he. "Yes," I said oozing nonchalance, "Is that so strange?"

"Yes." "No." They answered in unison. "Oh boy," said my youngest, "Okay Sis, we better set mom straight on a few things." (HE was going to set ME straight?) "First of all, look out for the old yawn trick—you know, when he's sitting next to you and yawns and kind of stretches and then puts his arm around…."

"Don't tell me that corny technique is still being used," I asked, amusedly.

And you be sure to lock your own door," his sister chimed in, her face earnest.

"You mean when we get home?" I asked, puzzled.

"No. I mean in the car," she answered (no automatic door locks then). "I don't want him re-e-eaching across to lock your door (she demonstrated, sliding her hand across the front of my blouse).

"Yeah, and mom—" her brother started.

"Just a minute," I said exasperatedly, "I have something to ask **you.** If, when we get home, should he want to kiss me, *and*," I held up my hand to forestall their comments, should I want to let him, shall I run up and ask your permission first?" My eyes were beginning to narrow.

"Oh, hey, yeah, I'm glad you mentioned kissing," he interrupted.

"I wasn't serious!"

"NO, mom, this is really important," he was emphatic. "On *Love Boat*…"

"*Love Boat!*" I was incredulous. "What is this? The Gospel according to Gopher?"

"On *Love Boat*," he said firmly, ignoring my protests, "There's a kind of rule about kissing. There's a certain age--I don't know exactly what it is, but," looking straight at me seriously, "I know you're over it." My lips formed words, but no sound came out, and he continued. "When you get to this age, *you kiss with your mouth closed.*"

I couldn't believe it. I looked from one to the other, and

my irritation died. After all, they were just trying to help. I put my arms around them, and reassured them, "Look. I know how I felt about you both when you started to date and since this is kind of my first date I understand your concern." They looked relieved.

"Now I want to put your minds at ease." I smiled and they smiled back, not noticing the wicked gleam in my eye. "We may be a little late tonight, in case we decide to do something after the movie, but don't worry. I want you both to know that I won't do anything you wouldn't do."

Well. They very nearly locked me in my room. Children have NO sense of humor where parents and dating are concerned. I had to do some fast talking before my date arrived. I finally said, "Hey, mellow out." They seemed startled to hear *their* expression on *my* lips. "I'm just going out with a friend for dinner and dancing." That's exactly what it was, as I told them when I got home. It was pleasant, I enjoyed myself, and that was that.

That first date accomplished a lot, though. It was another step forward for me as an individual…not half of a couple. It was also the first time in months that THEY were both home before midnight on a Saturday night!

Say It with (Silk) Flowers

The biggest mistake couples make is to divide chores and never learn the other person's job. Not just because it limits one's capabilities, but because furniture, machinery and flowers can get used to one person's touch.

In *Cannery Row* John Steinbeck states that "Indeed there are men near whom a car runs better." It works in reverse too We had a stick-shift VW Bug that started hiccupping if I got within 6 feet of the driver's side of the car. However, I am the only person I know who **never** has an odd sock in the laundry basket. I **understand** the dryer. Once every full moon, I sacrifice one virgin sock and it's satisfied.

Machines have feelings, too. One man told me that right after his wife walked out the door, the dishwasher threw up. We have counseling for spouses and children, workshops for parents and teachers, but what about the fireplace? Do you think it belched soot in your face by accident? These things become **accustomed** to one person filling them...cleaning them...stoking them....

It's in the world of nature, however, that the loss of a familiar voice, a sure hand, a loving touch – is pitiful. Plants languish. Flowers develop blight. The very branches on the trees droop.

Enough movies have been made about men and women in traditional roles suddenly having to cope with **everything,** and the comical/disastrous results. Clichés can be tritely true (that's how they got to be clichés) and so can these stories. Many wives *are* innocents when it comes to cars, repairs and lawn care, just as many husbands *are* strangers to the sewing machine, food processor and laundry room. If their combined know-how knows how, what's the problem? I accepted certain work divisions without question. I didn't ask him to sew, he didn't ask me to mow.

Only a few people know the real reason he never asked me to do yard work. He loved his garden too much to expose it to my black thumb. Children, friendships, anything people related seem to flourish under my care, but I'm the unintentional Darth Vader of the greenhouse. Another friend, President of the Garden Club, dug some out of her back yard, brought it to mine and planted it in the best spot. She gave me some watering advice but said it needed almost no care. It died. Puzzled, she repeated the whole procedure. The same thing happened. She would sacrifice no more Cochia for me, telling me with incredulous exasperation that it was the first time she had known anyone to kill that plant. In fact, her neighbors had tried to **burn** it out of their yard without success. I think she exaggerated.

She had never treated me quite the same ever since I commented on one of her dead flower arrangements. Dead, dried, hey, they're not alive.

My hanging plants would go unremembered until I glanced up to see (remorsefully) yet one more ivy stiff with rigor mortis. There are cacti which can survive the blast-furnace heat and bitter cold of the desert, but not my window sill. I suffered massive guilt attacks. To atone, I bought spider plants and philodendron and vowed to water them regularly, writing myself notes, determined that **this** time would be different.

They didn't turn brown or get stiff, but they didn't look right, either. My friend came over (suspiciously) with her emergency bag of potting soil, plant food and vitamins, only to find that she was too late. Under my overzealous watering they had gone down for the third and last time. I dumped them all under the bushes. The limp yellow leaves and rotting roots reproached me silently. The deformed cactus went too, the spines giving me one last stab. After that, the only flora to be found in my house was silk.

Is it any wonder I was nervous when faced with the total responsibility of house **and** grounds? Up until then flowers, pants, shrubs, grass and trees had all been secure in the knowledge that they were in the hands of someone who understood them. Would they accept me when he was gone?

Again, I tried. With the kids' help, I mowed, trimmed,

weeded and watered. With growing confidence I would put the riding mower in fourth gear and slalom around the evergreens. I tipped my hat at a rakish angle and the very bees and butterflies seemed to know I meant business; everything hurried out of my way except for one toad that was either foreign or suicidal, because he dove under the wheel, ignoring my warning. All went well for awhile. In my naïveté I thought I was trusted. I forgot they had seen many plants suffer death at my hands. I was only tolerated. When they realized **he** wasn't coming back, they turned on me.

I was unaware of this at first, although it did seem that I received an inordinate number of scratches when trimming bushes no matter how careful I was. The lawn showed evidence of trauma by developing a kind of patchy acne. The hedges **deliberately** grew scraggly and uneven. The oak would lower its branches as if by accident when I mowed under it. It was the ivy, though, that caused me the most uneasiness. It grew thicker and denser, creeping up the house—becoming one with the screens. removing the paint when it was pulled off the wood, sneaking into the cellar windows when my back was turned. I slept fitfully, dreaming that I could hear it growing in the night. I awoke from these nightmares yelling, "Nuke the ivy! NUKE THE IVY!"

I kept things under control with weed-eater, clippers and mower, but I didn't kid myself. The word was out. (Talk about your grapevine!) I knew that one day I'd take my guitar and my leave, admitting defeat. You may see me, all dressed in black, singing, "I fought the lawn and the (strum!) lawn won! I fought the lawn and the (strum!) lawn won....

Transportation Trauma

I was 20 years old the last time I actually bought and paid for my own car. I didn't SELECT it all by myself, not knowing anything about used cars. My Uncle Joe, who did, accompanied me. He told me stories of used-car salesmen taking advantage of the young and innocent, luring them into buying by pointing out features like style and color while ignoring staid items like motors and tires. (That was years ago… I'm sure things are much different now.)

He warned me that they would tempt me into spending too much on a flashy make. You show me a person who thinks "image" "style" and "color" are not important in a car and I'll show you someone who has never owned a chartreuse Nash.

Uncle Joe cautioned me, before we started out, not to EVER get excited about a car in front of a salesman. ('Way back then, one had to be extremely careful.) So when he started bargaining he gave me a warning look, which I knew meant not to show any enthusiasm. I contained myself admirably as I gazed doubtfully at the florescent yellowish-green paint. (I've always been partial to blue.)

However, I didn't wish to seem ungrateful then, and I don't wish to now. The car had many positive points. The price was low enough so even I could afford it, the body, motor and tires were good, and I could never lose it in a parking lot. I know, I tried, often. On a clear day, I had only to look for the crowd. When the sun hit that brilliant neon color it gave off an almost radio-active glow, attracting the curious, the unbelieving, and usually one or two conscientious off-duty firemen. I sold it when I got married.

After that, I still never picked out a car, but was consulted as to color. Big concession. I remember the first new car we bought. That the designer had been permanently traumatized by old-fashioned bathtubs was evident. It was a popular import that had to be ordered 11 months in advance. I chose the color: midnight blue. When our name came up the car available was not the right color. We got a note from the dealer, saying it was pea-green. I felt selfish in insisting that we wait for my color selection so the children and I waited in anticipation while their father went to pick up our first, brand-new "pea-green" car.

Yes. Well. As he parked it proudly out front, I took a long, level look at it. Vegetables were definitely not what came to mind. That dealer was either color-blind or a **very** poor speller. We bought and sold many cars after that, and I had pretty much the same impact as to the color.

Years later I found myself in the position of having to buy a new car. On my own. My car, which should have been dubbed "Lazarus" because my son brought it to life so many times, was very ill.

I visited showrooms, alone or with friends. The salesmen were ESPECIALLY helpful when I was alone. One bruised his knee on a bumper in his haste to be of assistance. Another was so eager to help; he almost knocked his colleague over in his haste to get to me first. Each cautioned me against doing anything impulsive…except in HIS showroom. All were interested in my plight. One warned of the dangers of driving an old unreliable car, truly distressed to think it might break down, leaving me stranded in icy weather. Winters in upstate New York were challenging. I listened to all of them politely, but even after all those years I remembered my uncle's warnings. (Even though they were completely without warrant, I'm sure)

I read up on the various makes and models, asked opinions, and steadfastly wavered. Finally I picked one, but there was a three-month waiting list and my car was on its last (bald) tires. Happily, I got the opportunity to buy the make I wanted when someone's deal didn't go through. No choice of color or options, though, they were already chosen. I made a decision (still a novelty for me), and bought it, becoming a new member of the "page-of-the-month" book club.

I loved my new car. The color? Color isn't everything, you know. However, I must confess to a certain smugness when I tell you it perfectly matched Melissa Manchester's old hit…"Midnight Blue!"

The Ultimate Night Out

I have it all planned, beginning with breakfast in bed and finishing with…no, I won't jump to the end so quickly. I'll take you along on my evening out.

Of course I sleep in, and the fact that it is Friday just adds that extra fillip to my pleasure. It's almost un-American not to snooze a bit later on weekends (except for those poor unfortunates who are born with binoculars, putters or fishing poles attached to their hands) but Fridays…Fridays are pure indulgence.

This morning lazily drags its heels into afternoon, as I finally waken to breathe the breakfast provided by—who else? "Breakfast in Bed" caterers, naturally. A perfect rose, (real, of course), a choice of four kinds of coffee, freshly ground on the premises, hand-squeezed orange juice, fresh fruit, hot croissants, delicate and flaky, and eggs, prepared to my liking. To me the obvious choice is coddled eggs, as gently coddled as I feel. The piece de resistance is flambéed crepes served with a flourish by skillful chefs, attired in tails, of course. I sip a little champagne, now and then, blissfully finishing my breakfast.

The limousine isn't due for two or three hours. Plenty of time to get ready, although my hair stylist does not like to be rushed. He's making a house call...unheard of for him...until now.

A friend will accompany me on this special evening. I feel it should be shared to be fully savored. We are driven to an elegant beach hotel for a "Lakeside Delight", a choice of fresh strawberry or banana daiquiris, various exotic coffees and desserts. Part of the "Delight" is to sip them on the veranda, as we enjoy the view of the lake.

We ride out to a downtown hotel for cocktails, arriving just as the trio plays light jazz for the "tea dances". These dances are so named because in the past, from 5:30 to 8PM, society often paused for a cup of tea, or perhaps a stronger libation. They are also reminiscent of those dances held during Prohibition, when drinks were served in teacups to disguise the contents. Much more genteel than drinking from a lady's dancing slipper, don't you think?

The windows on three sides create a greenhouse effect. They overlook the city from the ninth floor, commanding an excellent view of the city skyline. The shrimp and crab claws served us are fresh, and whet our appetites for dinner ahead.

Ordinarily we would stay to the end, but tonight our chauffeur is waiting to drive us out to the airport. We have chartered a helicopter to take us over the city...

it's almost dusk as we become airborne. The sun, low in the sky, turns brighter; it looks like a florescent pumpkin, coloring the wisps of clouds around it. It seems to hang on the horizon, motionless, and then, suddenly, it's gone. It's that time between day and night when everything looks charcoal grey, and the buildings below us seem to blur into each other.

The lights of the city go on, gradually at first, then in clusters…neons, streetlights, shop windows, restaurants and high rises become visible, as the city dons her jewels. The sky darkens dramatically, in a hurry to show off its lights too? as if in response to those below.

We're back at the airport, and on our way to dinner almost too soon. It was difficult to choose only one restaurant, with so many excellent ones available, but I finally decided on Le Champignon, where the cuisine is impeccable. Fresh flowers on the table, subdued lighting and the lovely artwork all contribute to its quiet elegance.

We're served marinated mushrooms, compliments of the chef, as we glance at the menu. I was already fairly certain of our choice: Chateaubriand for two. Our personal guide during this gastronomic delight smiles her approval. We ask her to recommend a wine to complement our dinner. She selects a 1964 vin de Chateau Latour…a **most** suitable wine. Not wanting to spoil our now keen appetites with too heavy an appetizer, we decide to split an order of escargots between us. The sauce, with its subtle garlic flavor, sets them off deliciously. The salad is crisp, the herbed tomatoes perfectly done and the pommes frites—potatoes soaked in ice water to remove the extra starch, then crisply fried—were excellent. The Chateaubriand…simply superb. It's sliced for us, the knife cutting effortlessly through the meat. We are NOT disappointed in our choice.

The desserts offered are tempting, but we decide on just coffee. Of course, it isn't **just** coffee, it's Irish Coffee. I've never had coffee served quite like this before. It's almost as great a pleasure to watch it being prepared as to drink it. ALMOST. First she takes fresh orange wedges and coats the goblets with the juice, running the wedges around the rims. Then she pours 151-proof rum in each glass, touching a flame to one. She lights the second glass from the first. Gracefully, skillfully, she turns the goblets from side to side, around and around, the blue flame softly dancing, 'til the sugar is caramelized around the rims. Then Irish whiskey and rich coffee are poured in and topped with fresh whipped cream. We smile in appreciation as we sip the liquid through the cream. It's coffee and dessert in one—truly a fitting finish to the meal.

Dance! That's what I want to do now. The night life at Truffles Bar, with its "marquee" lighting will be in full swing, and I want to be part of it. The music is a nice mixture of fast and slow, everything the crowd enjoys, and there **is** a good crowd. The band stops around 1:30 and we linger a bit, but we're not ready to wind down yet.

The air smells fresh to us as we walk to our waiting limo, the chauffeur smiling as he helps us in the car.

He heads for the lake, to the Yacht Club, where friends have invited us for a champagne breakfast. Our gourmet dinner is history after all that exercise, and breakfast sounds good. (After all, we never **did** have dessert.)

The 40-foot Chris Craft looks very romantic as we walk down the pier. The cabin is lit with candlelight from hurricane lamps, protected from the breeze. From the galley comes the aroma of bacon and coffee. Champagne is cooling in the bucket. The morning air puts an edge on our appetite. There are fluffy omelets, tiny fruit and cheese-filled pastries, sausage strata; layers of thinly sliced bread and meat, cream, eggs and cheese, with servings of home fries for the heartier appetites.

We cruise down the lake and back as we breakfast from a dainty table set with silver and lace. We're an intimate little group, six in all. It's a pleasure to chat companionably with friends in a normal voice after talking over the band music. The boat is docked, the conversation becomes quieter as we sip one more cup of coffee. The warmth of it feels good to us as the air cools down a bit.

The yacht sleeps six and we are invited to stay, but we decline with warm thanks. Our driver, a friend by now, has had a little nap after his hearty breakfast in the galley. Dawn is close at hand and we have one more thing to do. Our shoes click on the pier as we walk back, the sound carrying over the water.

Our driver has his orders, and we head back toward the city, stopping at a large deserted field. My friend and I get out of the limo, wrapping our sweaters around us. We grin excitedly as we watch the hot air balloon filling. The pilot motions us over and we climb in the basket. It's almost full now, gently tugging at the restraining ropes. The ground crew unties the ropes and the huge balloon rises slowly. The sky is getting lighter in the East as we float higher…higher…over houses and trees. It's quiet, except for the noise when the propane is turned on.

Our mood is peaceful and serene as we watch the sun rise. It's spectacular—a deeper red than we saw it set—how many hours ago? Eight? Nine? We waft over the countryside, taking it all in…horses, cows, and deer leaping gracefully. Occasionally a dog would bark, spooked by the "whoosh" of the propane.

There's the city skyline again, not the soft charcoal color of last night, but as crisp and businesslike as a freshly folded morning paper. It's time to come back to earth again, back to our daily living, but our pilot brings us down gently, without too harsh a jolt of reality.

Our chauffeur and the ground crew have been following us, although we floated in a straight line and they had to abide by road and traffic rules. We bid our pilot adieu in the now-bright dawn, climb into the limo and head back to the city, tired now, but with the magic of the evening's events still with us. It has indeed been the ultimate night out.

Full House

Looking back, it seems as if our house was always overflowing with children…our own five, their friends, "Fresh Air" children and all the noise, fun and clutter that goes with them. I knew someday they would leave, and prepared myself accordingly, I thought. In my case, however every time I braced myself for the "empty nest" syndrome, the nest got crowded again. Once out of high school, my kids left all right, but they kept coming back.

The oldest girl went to college coming home summers. My oldest son got a job ad went in on an apartment with a friend, only to come back home after a year. My second daughter went to college for a year, then started working and living in an apartment with a friend. Their younger sister followed suit, working and living in an apartment with a friend, when the second one came home for awhile, then both of them left. Confused? You bet I was! We were the only family on the block with a revolving front door.

Somewhere in there the oldest son and daughter left to get married (to two other people). They never came back to live. then my youngest son and his friend, who had been living with us for the summer, both went away to college. In the midst of this, my husband, who REALLY must've gotten caught up into the swing of things, also left. He never came back either. Not even for visits.

Now. If you've made any sense of all this, you know that except when my youngest boy came home for Christmas and summer vacation, the only inhabitants of the house were me and our dog Truffles. Did I forget to mention her? If you HAVE made some sense of all this, I wish you'd explain it to me.

The large house and lot were a bit much for only one person to handle. Forget Truffles...she never so much as picked up a dishtowel...NEVER carried her share of the load—so to speak. Nine rooms and an acre of land were about twice what I needed which was fine, actually, since I only owned half the property anyway. The person who owned the other half had since become someone else's "other half". Half the house, half the land.... I considered settling the whole thing with a tape measure and a saw, starting with the trees...the top half.

Well. Such a fuss over a couple of trees. Not even my lawyer understood. He convinced me that the best solution would be to simply sell the house. I knew he was right, but as I wandered through the house, I found myself getting more and more depressed. Could it be that "empty-nest" syndrome had caught me off guard? It didn't make sense to me because I was *happy* for my kids. Some were married with families, some living with roommates or in college…also, I admitted, it was time for me to move into a smaller place. I'd like that.

Then what was the matter? As I walked from room to room, gazing despondently, tears on my face, I realized what the problem was. It was NOT "empty-nest" syndrome, as I had feared. The trouble was that the nest was anything but empty! It was crammed with years of "Mom, can I leave this for now?" Or "Mom, can I store this until?" The clutter that had accumulated was overwhelming! The thought of disposing of all that stuff would send **anyone** into a depression.

"Simply sell the house, HAH!" Prospective buyers would have to actually go through and LOOK at everything. Everything, including CLOSETS which still harbored kids' clothes, books, stuffed animals and games. The GARAGE, which held, besides lawn equipment, tires from three different cars, including one for which we had held funeral services years ago, an old console TV, three-quarters of two bicycles, some ancient roller skates, chipped flower pots and a couple of taped-up hockey sticks. The rest of the stuff was just junk.

The CELLAR! I made myself take inventory. Uh-oh, worse even than I had feared. It was crammed with decrepit pool and ping-pong tables, odd cans of dried-up paint, roll-away bed with no mattress, (no wheels, either, which I guess made it a carry-away), weights, boxes of old 78rpm records (how many of you know what those are?), odd boots, and an immensely heavy old bureau, sans mirror, that was left by the people WE bought the house from. What to do?

GARAGE SALE! I forgot who first mentioned it to me, but it seemed the perfect solution. Yes. Well. Someday, when I can recall getting ready for, and actually **holding** my garage sale without coming down with a case of shingles, I will fulfill a goal in life and warn innocent people of the hazards involved.

All I could (greedily) think of at the time, though, was that empty nest! I mean **really** empty! Closets where clothes could hang…straight up and down! A garage that I could, in fact, drive a car **into**! Actually being able to get to my washer and dryer without the use of rope and piton!

Had I known what was in store for me, I would have done the only sensible thing: sealed off the house, and become a permanent groupie for Neil Diamond.

'Tis the Season

I love holidays. Baking (and eating!), shopping, caroling, candlelight and prayers…but that year it was no ordinary season.

I was getting ready to move, but could not seem to pin anyone (lawyer, banker, builder) down as to **when**. Having a nervous breakdown sounded heavenly, but I didn't have **time**! I was Activities Director for an organization during this busy time of the year. There were meetings and newsletters, social events which involved toting paper goods, coffee, food, etc., as well as arranging all the events in the first place.

My car, which had been ailing for some time became deathly ill when I really needed it. AND, I was packing, *packing,* **PACKING!** How could I have so much stuff left after giving furniture to my kids, holding the garage sale, donating to schools and charities…I'm sure the two Volunteers of America developed hernias after carting tons of stuff away, but still my fingers were charcoal from news print as I continued the endless wrapping.

While filling one box I spotted just the right thing to

fill the box: a box of chocolates still in the cellophane. I wrapped newspaper around it, tucked it in and sealed the box. (A tasty surprise for some nice unpacker.) Questions beset me as I worked. Where should we plan Christmas dinner? Should I buy a tree? What about decorations? Could I even *find* them? When would I rewrite my January column? Was the car going to make it? Merciful heavens, was *I* going to make it?

My editors thought the column should be more uplifting, giving heart and courage to those facing the holidays alone. Understandably, I was leaning the other way, towards togetherness; if you're going into a depression, why go alone? Take a few friends along. The more the merrier. Well. So to speak.

One night I took what I thought was the "activities box" to a meeting, only to discover I had mistakenly brought my best stemware (packed beautifully, of course). A friend drove me back to exchange boxes. I stopped short in alarm when I entered the house. A box was in shreds, books and papers scattered everywhere on the floor. I froze, listening fearfully, only my eyes moving, afraid I had interrupted a burglar.

Then I saw the thief, peering out guiltily from under the coffee table: our beagle Truffles, with telltale bits of foil at the corner of her mouth. The kitchen door had evidently come unlatched. She had gotten into the living room and sniffed out the chocolates. Unbelievable. That candy was unopened, cellophaned, newspaper wrapped, and sealed in a cardboard box, yet she got to it. (When it came to food, Truffles was an animal.) Amid the litter were four untouched chocolates; orange creams. I hate orange creams. There was cardboard confetti on my floor and murder in my eyes. The dog, sensing that her life was in serious danger, streaked for the basement, and wisely stayed there. I sent my friend back with the right box, and gazed at the mess.

All of a sudden, I was bone tired. The fears and doubts I had kept pushed down under the weight of all the activity and problems ballooning up caught me off-guard. I was frightened because so much needed doing, and where were my energy and efficiency? I was frightened because I was leaving my home…except that it wasn't mine anymore, it was someone else's. But the one I was moving into certainly wasn't mine, either. It wasn't anyone's yet. It was blank off-white walls, rooms with no memories…pristine carpeting…an oven that hadn't baked a cookie How could I call it home? Was I making a mistake?

The phone rang. One of my daughters had called to ask how I was doing, and if I had finished my gift shopping. FINISHED! Dear Lord, I hadn't bought one thing yet. "Everything's great, except that Truffles is sabotaging what packing I *do* get done, my deadlines have caught up with me and I haven't even STARTED shopping. I'd run away from home if I could decide which home to run away *from*, because I don't see how I'm going to get everything *done*." I meant to sound flippant, but the panic must've broken through.

"Mom. The Christmas season should NOT make your life more difficult. It should be the best time of the year, not a chore. If you want, I can do your shopping right along with mine, but the gifts are not important. The important thing is that we'll be together." My voice wobbled a bit as I tried to quip, "Out of the mouths of babes."

Well, I did only a tiny fraction of my usual shopping that year. I gave mostly money, and they had a good time shopping together, picking out exactly what they wanted for themselves, children, husbands and boyfriends. I was *delighted* with the gifts I gave them. I didn't send out one card (no email, then) or cut out one cookie.

Next year will not be so busy; I'll have time to make the holidays special and personal. **In my new home.**

Another Happy New Year!

Remember Al Capp's comic strip Li'l Abner?" At the end of every year it was the same; the New Year Baby, literally ready to take on the world, with big plans, anxious to get started, enthusiastic about the months ahead, smiling, innocent, idealistic… kind of like what newlyweds look like in the early days of marriage.

Then there was the Old Year, who just wanted *out* – scraggly bearded, bent and beaten, unbelievably exhausted, disillusioned, cynical…. Yes. Well. Some years are harder to celebrate then others.

New Year's Eve is supposed to be a happy time, but can be depressing if you miss someone. After the divorce, friends inquired about my holiday plans. Since Christmas, New Year's and our anniversary all fell within three weeks of each other, I could understand their solicitude, but shrugged it off, amusedly. I felt a little sorry for women who had to plan to be busy so they wouldn't get lonely, but solved that one by planning to spend it the way I always had.

"With your EX?" They laughed, but I was serious. After

all, we had spent every New Year's Eve together for the past 25 years. Why should this one be any different? So what if he had someone else? He could leave her at home and spend the holiday with me. There were many times when he left me at home and spent the holiday with her. Fair is fair. Just to be sure, though, I'd ask him about New Year's when I called to firm up plans for our anniversary.

You know he didn't see it that way? The man simply has no sense of tradition. Not only was he unreasonable, he was downright rude; said I was crazy to even think we'd spend the holiday together. Then *I* got angry and said, "Fine! Then you can just celebrate our anniversary without me!" He said "WHAT?"

"That's right," I said nastily, "AND, you can just forget about your Christmas gift!" Boy, talk about tough. Too bad if I was hard on him. Sometimes you have to take a firm stand. I don't know…things just haven't been the same since the divorce.

On what would have been our anniversary I went to dinner and a movie with a friend. She and I had a great time. I had seen comedies before, of course, but it was a brand new experience enjoying one with someone who has a sense of humor.

Christmas was tougher, I won't lie to you, but I kept busy with shopping, baking and holiday get-togethers. If I started to feel sorry for myself, determination (and some residual anger) steered me away from it. Between Christmas Eve at my folks, midnight Mass with the kids and a big Christmas dinner surrounded by family, I found a lot to be thankful for.

That darned New Year's Eve thing kept cropping up, though. It had always been a big thing with us – the party at my folks', friends, music, fun.... To tell the truth, I simply could not imagine a New Year's Eve without good ol' "what's-his-name," any more than I could imagine Guy Lombardo's band not playing *Auld Lang Syne* at the Roosevelt Hotel in New York City. I heard that they still did, even though he passed on. Okay, if they could go on without him, I could go to the party alone. I'd start a NEW tradition.

We danced and sang and I had a *good* time. We made our own music with guitars, piano, banjo and a slide trombone that would knock your socks off. Just before midnight I played the piano as we sang *Auld Lang Syne*. I could feel the hands of friends on my shoulders. When I stood and faced everyone, I got the impression that the whole room was moving toward me. It was as if they all had the same idea, "Don't let Lorraine be alone at midnight." I could feel love with every hug. My brother said, holding me tightly, "Remember Sis, we're a close family, but when anyone wants to come in, we let them. If they don't want us, we don't need them."

Well. We partied a couple of hours more before winding it up. The weather was freezing, and I shivered as I drove home alone. I had to get out of the car to raise the garage door, and my eyes watered from the cold. It really was bitter. I wiped them dry, but they continued. The house seemed bigger, quieter than usual.

Still shivering, I turned the heat up and wrapped up in an afghan, trying to get warm. My eyes kept watering, probably from having contacts in too long, and from the cigarette smoke.

I thought about the party again, remembering those waves of love that had surrounded me at midnight, my brother's words, and reminded myself how lucky I was. I wondered if Guy Lombardo's band still does perform on New Year's Eve even though he's gone. Actually, they do, and so do I.

A Moving Experience

Often when we go through traumatic experiences we get support and sympathy from unexpected sources, No sooner did I start to look at various types of housing than I began to hear from moving companies. They offered their assistance even before my friends did! They sent postcards offering their services, and letters saying they wanted to take the stress out of my move. They telephoned, "Lorraine, please let us help you." One message said, "All we hope for is the opportunity to relocate the treasures of your world." (Wouldn't you just bet that someone in that organization had just taken a creative writing course?)

My fears about my pictures, mirrors and piano being damaged started melting away. I was truly touched. I didn't even know they cared! I read through all the literature, trying to decide on the best company. They were as varied as TV shows. One made choosing sound like a game, offering "Clues to look for when looking for a mover."Another took a medical viewpoint, insisting they were "Just what the doctor ordered." Spoonful of Sugar Van Lines, I believe that was.

One had an excellent reputation for reliability, careful handling, courtesy, promptness and old-fashioned concern. I think that was the company run by former Eagle Scouts. The extremely cagey one couldn't be pinned down—"Probable cost of transportation, estimated charge for containers, probable cost of packing and unpacking services, finally totaling up to 'The total probable cost estimate.' " (I estimated there was a strong possibility that I would choose another company.)

One emphasized the trust factor, and referred me to their "moving counselor". Space-age efficiency was evident in one company's Countdown Kit" starting six weeks before moving day. First instruction: "Choose your moving company" – logical. The countdown continued from week to week to the day before to Ta-daa – M-Day. (Plan to eat out today.) One mover offered to take special care of my mirrors for only $75 extra. That almost sounded like blackmail.

Suggestions for an "Adventure Kit" sounded romantic. I felt like a pilgrim, for some reason. Then disillusionment set in when I read the first item on the list: Aspirin. So much for romance. An efficient one warned me to "Have prescriptions filled before you leave". Some suggestions insinuated that I wasn't too bright: "Do your laundry before movers arrive". (Duh?) And of course: "If closing your bank account, BE SURE TO KEEP ENOUGH MONEY TO PAY THE DRIVER." They all had advice to this effect.

The one that recommended a "well-organized adventure" ended with this advice: "Pay moving charges (fools these people are NOT), make the beds so you can get some rest and do not use your TV, washer or dishwasher for 24 hours". Naturally, they don't come right out and SAY that's how long you'll sleep from exhaustion. I liked the reassurance of care all the movers gave (maybe not the mirror one), the feeling of *security*... that all my household goods would be *in good hands*—or, wait a minute—maybe I was thinking of my car....

I picked the one I thought was best. The representative began talking about insurance, explaining that movers are required by law to carry a minimum amount per pound. I'm sure that's a good law but I smiled smugly in the knowledge that MY mover's safety record was impressive. Then he gently pointed out that this minimum amount would not be much for a heavy item. Wait! What heavy item? Couch? Dining room table? PIANO? Hey! They had carried pioneer's belongings west, and moved museum treasures—delicate scientific equipment with nary a jostle...uh, hadn't they?

He immediately reassured me, saying of course nothing would happen but IF a mishap should occur, WHICH WAS HIGHLY UNLIKELY, I could buy the depreciated Value Protection which would pay a little more. However, the **Replacement Cost Protection** would insure that I would be reimbursed whatever it cost to replace the item. This was the best coverage. (Also the most expensive.) He left me pamphlets titled, "Your rights and responsibilities when you move" and

"Household Goods Dispute Settlement Program" telling me to let him know my decision. The pamphlets expounded on arbitration… claims… legalities…. I sat looking at my piano in consternation. Just when I thought it was safe for my household treasures to be carried out into the highway traffic once more…

Now I know why the first thing in that "Adventure Kit" was Aspirin.

Show Place

The garage sale, like a tornado, had taken many household items with it. The usual flotsam remained (the jetsam sold the first hour) along with one big item: The basement still held the big dresser (sans mirror) that had been left by the people who sold us the house. I had been trying to get rid of it ever since we moved in, but there it stood.

One bedroom was completely empty. Even the closet! (How 'bout **that**?) Truffles couldn't understand why she couldn't have her own bedroom now that we didn't have standing room only. It's my fault. I never could bring myself to tell her a vital fact of life: that she's a beagle. My "other son" (no relation, but he and my son were like brothers) would warn me, "Ma, she's gotta know someday," and told her heartlessly, "Truff, you're a dog. You've always been a dog and you'll always be a dog." She looked at me for denial, and I could never quite meet her eyes.

It was marvelous to have an uncluttered house, though. I went through the rooms with satisfaction until I came to the basement. I looked at the dresser, speculatively.

No one wanted to buy it. Of course, none of the potential buyers had been amazons, either. It was a massive piece of furniture; I decided to donate it to charity along with everything else that didn't sell. Two men arrived the following Friday and looked sadly at the boxes labeled "books". "You got mostly books?" asked the first one. "Heavy," said the other. They brightened considerably when they saw the lighter weight items like clothes, toys and games. I said there was one piece of furniture in the basement, which they said they'd load last. When I took them downstairs and showed them the dresser, their faces saddened again. One man gave it an experimental shove. It didn't move. His partner tried pushing harder. The dresser gave half an inch. I suggested taking the drawers first, to lighten the load, then the frame. They each removed one, hefting them gingerly. I asked anxiously if they could handle it. They assured me that it was no problem. I left them to it. It wasn't a problem, either. Not to them. They handled it quickly and efficiently. **Very quickly**. They loaded those two drawers, and speedily took off before I realized what they were doing. I ran out, but it was too late. They were history. I bet that guy used to drive getaway cars.

I stamped down the cellar stairs and, sure enough, there it stood, defiantly, looking heavier and more massive than ever in spite of the missing mirror and now, two missing drawers. I regarded it uneasily, thinking of how my many attempts to get rid of it had been thwarted. Couldn't sell it, couldn't give it away…maybe I could **throw** it away. I decided to wait (I had a choice?)

until the house was sold and have my movers take it out to the curb. If they could handle freezers and pianos they could handle this, I reasoned, but without real conviction. Maybe I had seen too many Vincent Price movies, but I was beginning to really hate that dresser.

With help, I got the house ready to "show". The first open house was like a coming-out party. The house was all spruced up, ready for people to come and admire. Inside it was polished, perfumed (I had just baked) and sparkling. Outside, the grounds were trimmed, raked and manicured. It was left in the capable hands of my realtor who assured me he valued it like his own.

That first Sunday was just the beginning. Real estate agents called constantly with questions: Did I have a brook? Her client wanted a babbling brook. I had a pond. I explained, with dignity, that ponds do not babble. Ponds have *always* been more self-contained than brooks.

It was a necessary invasion of privacy. Everything **always** had to look like a showplace. I would bake something if there was time, remembering my broker's instructions: "There's nothing like the aroma of freshly baked goods as the people are walking through an immaculate, bright house." I would check everything before anyone arrived, reciting, "Lights turned UP, lids turned DOWN. (You know the lids I'm talking about.) Then the dog and I would go for a walk as agents took their prospective buyers through. Truffles and I ate a lot of cake during that time. We walked a lot of miles, too, which was just as well because we *really* ate a lot of cake.

In a surprisingly short time I got the phone call: "Your house has been sold." I was elated. No more holding open houses! No more strangers tramping through! No more phone calls from realtors! I could say goodbye (and good riddance!) to that dresser in the basement! My house had been sold! No more responsibility of the large house…no more caring and feeding and landscaping that acre of lawn.

No more boating on that beautiful pond in the summer…no more more ice-skating on it in the winter…. I would no longer see that lovely view each day, or have spontaneous over-the-fence visits with these neighbors who had become warm supportive friends… **My home had been sold.**

Sprinklers and Saints

I moved into a town house. Yes! No yard work or landscaping. There were few pet restrictions, too which was important to me. I saw people walking Toy Poodles, Shiatsus, Peke-a-Poos, etc. They all looked like they had just stepped out of a fashion magazine; every hair in place…the owners were very well-groomed, too. Not a mutt showed its face. Maybe they had to be walked at night. (Some associations were strict.)

I would casually mention that my dog had a pedigree. She comes from a long line of champions. You can almost smell the Wheaties on her breath. Somehow people would get the idea that she was a dainty French poodle. Probably because of her name: Truffles. I never had the heart to tell anyone she was a fat, friendly beagle. Shoot, I never even had the heart to tell *Truffles* that.

The townhouse was a modest one—no pool, clubhouse or gazebo. (I adore gazebos.) However, a no-nonsense, sturdy deck would have to do. The maintenance fee was well below average. Then I learned why. I would, in fact, have to take care of my lawn. The builders would do the initial landscaping and seeding but after that it would be up to me. ME, the Attila the Hun of the plant kingdom...ME, the terror of the green world, ME, the.... Oh, this was not good.

I learned one definite fact: Mother Nature had put me on the naughty list long ago, and she had a memory like a steel trap. As soon as spring arrived, it rained unrelentingly on the frozen ground. There was no grass yet, just dirt, which eventually became a thick, oozy brown. Driveway (unpaved, as yet) sidewalk and yard all took on the same shade of mud. It was a major deterrent for visitors.

Finally it cleared up long enough for the workmen to grade and seed Soon I could distinguish between the lawn and driveway and my sidewalk appeared again. It even dried up enough for me to walk to the mailbox in sneakers instead of "duck boots". It got drier...and drier...and drier until deep cracks began forming in the soil. After rescuing a few stray balls and one adventurous kitten, it dawned on me that the lawn probably needed water. Hah! Here was my chance to get on the good side of Mother Nature and, incidentally, grow a nice lawn. (Always the optimist.) After starting the sprinkler I decided to take Truffles for a walk and familiarize myself with the neighborhood.

Almost every driveway had a car in it and I remember wondering why people didn't keep them in their garages. I went by one driveway in which were parked two Volkswagens. Then I noticed one of them had paws instead of wheels. There, tied to that VW Bug, stood the biggest St. Bernard I had ever seen. I'm talking **massive** here.

Remember the classic picture of the St. Bernard standing over people he found in the snow? That huge, loveable good-natured best friend of man with that little keg of brandy around his neck, to revive lost travelers? I have my own theory why these St. Bernards were good-natured. The next time you see one of those pictures, take a good look at the dog—a really **close** look. Note the mouth hanging open…slobbering gently… eyes slightly out of focus…. Isn't its whole demeanor strongly reminiscent of a college junior during spring break? You can't convince ME the dogs didn't come in for their share of the booze.

Have you never wondered what happens to these dogs when they're no longer required to save frozen travelers AND celebrate with them? Have you never thought about how nasty withdrawal can make them? I never did, either, until I found myself staring one in the face.

He leaped at us, growling and tugging at his rope. I turned to run, but Truffles wanted to play with him! I was panicking as I dragged her the opposite way. He opened his mouth, letting out an angry howl that shattered the right headlight of the car. With alarm I saw the VW start to shudder. I picked Truffles up (no easy task—she was built like a fire hydrant) and was desperately trying to get her home, but made a wrong turn and couldn't tell which house was mine.

I ran in a half-crouch, struggling with the squirming, indignant dog. (She didn't seem to understand that you just don't FROLIC with King Kong.) I realized, too late, what all my neighbors already knew: It's easier to recognize your CAR than your house. And I had foolishly, **foolishly** parked my car in the garage.

Well. I found the house, of course. It was the only one without numbers on it. The first thing I did was put the house numbers up. No, that's the second thing. The first thing I did was park my car in my driveway.

Sipping a cup of tea to soothe my nerves, I heard water running. The sprinkler! I made my way to the faucet hoping I wouldn't slide down the slight slope. No worries. You can't slide when you're ankle deep in mud. I made my way to the steps and sat, contemplating the mud I used to call shoes. I reflected on the ironies of life, remembering the main reason I chose townhouse living was because I thought someone else would be responsible for outside maintenance. And the other reason? Oh yes, of course. There were no pet restrictions.

She Floats Through the Air....

Ever since I can remember, I've always wanted to fly. I had dreams about being airborne. I still remember a dream I had as a little girl: I was at the top of a high staircase. I jumped, and floated down. I can still remember the feeling. I'm here to tell you about how I celebrated my 70th year by jumping out of a perfectly good airplane, and what adventures led up to that point.

When my son George was 18, he started skydiving. The first time he did, I asked him to please call me and tell me how he liked it. He grinned at me knowingly, and said, "You just want to hear my voice, don't you?" I nodded sheepishly. Yes. Well. He called me, and when I asked how it was, he said, "Oh ma, it was unbelievable!" I thought, shoot, now he's going to want to go all the time. I was right, of course. It was a real challenge to me, as his mother, to watch him take off on his motorcycle to go skydiving. But I will tell you, part of me was a little envious. How I would like to experience that!

When George turned 21 we celebrated our birthdays by

going up in a hot air balloon. He's like his mom…he likes heights too. Family and friends turned out to see us off. My brother Nick took one look at the balloon laid out on the ground and said worriedly, "Honey, that balloon has a hole in it!" Well it did. They all do. There has to be an opening [gesture with "praying" hands] to let hot air out when descending.

George and I grinned at each other excitedly as the balloon gently started rising. My 3 year old granddaughter, sitting on the hood of their car with her mother's arms around her watched and waved as we floated higher and higher waving, "'Bye daddy… 'Bye grandma…" like the munchkins in "The Wizard of Oz". We watched the panorama open below. It was peaceful—silent except when the sound of the propane spooked three horses and dogs. An hour later when we gently alit I knew I would have to do it again.

I got the opportunity when on vacation with three other women just outside Phoenix, AZ. I had made all the arrangements before we even left home. We were picked up before sunrise. Hot-air balloons typically go up at sunrise or sunset; when there is the least breeze. There we were, four women in the back of a truck, in the dark, being driven somewhere by a man we had never seen before. One of my friends said, "Hey, who is this guy, and how did he know where to pick us up? She seemed relieved when she heard that his company was listed in the AAA Travel Book. The sky lightened just as the balloons went up…three in all. We saw the sun rise over Oak Creek Canyon as we drifted gently, enjoying the view, then descended to a champagne breakfast. Lovely.

Parasailing was next! My youngest son Rob and I were vacationing in Key West when we saw the parachutes going up—and down. I offered to take us both, but being high over the ocean tethered to a boat was definitely NOT his cup of tea. The man before me was fairly thickset and they landed him light as a feather so I had no qualms. What a rush it was when I took off. It was almost like flying to me. Midway through the ride they lowered me down so my feet touched the ocean, then that RUSH! as I took off again. Rob said later that everyone kind of chuckled when I took off. I weighed about 95 pounds. He said everyone else rose gently in a slow arc, but I went almost straight up! I went parasailing again in Bermuda with my nephew. Our car looked something like a small Ferris wheel car. It was fun of course, but more like an exciting ride than flying.

Years later I flew to San Diego to visit Rob. He always had some neat choices of things I might like to do, like the parasailing in Key West. This visit he suggested a glider. Absolutely. I'd like to try that. I asked him if he would like to go, too…my treat. He wouldn't be out in the open, but inside the plane. He had been in planes countless times. He thought about it, and said, "Yeah, okay, I'll go."

There wasn't a whole lot of room in the back seat of the glider, but neither of us was very big. Well, after a while, it started to get a little close in there. He tried to take his jacket off but there wasn't enough room in which to maneuver. I was enjoying our adventure but he was becoming more and more uneasy. I glanced surreptitiously over at him occasionally and noticed him perspiring, but didn't want to make a big deal of it. [Pause…] Then he threw up. We eventually landed, and thanked the pilot. Rob was kind of quiet. I told him I was sorry he didn't enjoy the ride. He wasn't upset with me but really didn't want to talk about it. I never knew what a horrible experience it was for him until we were at our family reunion later that summer.

My daughter Audrey said, "Hey, you guys went up in a glider, huh? I want to hear all about it." I said, "Oh Audrey, it was great! There were two planes, our glider in the back, and the plane with the engine in the front." Rob said, "Yeah mom, I gotta tell you, I really prefer my planes to have engines in them!" Then I said, "Anyway, the pilot in the first plane starts the engine. Then they connect the two planes with a cable." Rob said, "Cable! "A CABLE! Mom, did you even look at it? That wasn't a cable, it was a flippin' piece of TWINE!"

Audrey was having trouble keeping a straight face. I just shook my head and went on. "The plane took us up – I don't know, maybe 2000 feet? As soon as we were high enough so our pilot could fly on the currents, he detached the cable connecting us to the other plane." Rob said, "And that was ANOTHER thing! I had to watch our umbilical cord just…drifting away!"

I told her the pilot started telling us different facts, I'm sure trying to make it more interesting for Rob…what the name of that mountain in the distance was.... Rob said, "Yeah. Audrey, he's telling us that mountain is six miles away. ONLY SIX MILES AWAY? One good gust of wind and BAM! we're on the six o'clock news! I'm looking down and I can't see the runway, I can't see buildings, I can't see ANYTHING but hard ground. How are we going to get back to the airport? And if we do get back how is he going to slow down and LAND this sucker? WITHOUT AN ENGINE!"

And there's our mother, sitting there, smiling, nodding her head and saying, 'Mm-hmm, Mm-hmm". I gotta tell you, sis - there's something wrong with mom. She simply doesn't worry about these things. She—she's just not RIGHT."

By this time Audrey couldn't stop laughing. She said, "Oh brother! Were you guys even on the same plane together?"

You know, I was beginning to wonder myself. We had shared the exact same experience, yet his was awful, and I'd do it again in a heartbeat. See, I don't think I'm foolhardy, I just like to try new things.

There's a saying I like. "Never be afraid to try something new. Just remember: amateurs built the Ark; professionals built the Titanic."

I once read about a man and woman sitting next to each other on a plane. Just before takeoff he noticed her knuckles were white from gripping the arm rests. He saw that she was definitely a senior, and definitely scared. He asked what the problem was. She said she was terrified…that the plane could crash, or catch on fire, or…and she went on until he interrupted her and calmed her down, telling her that airplane travel was actually one of the safest modes of transportation. You know, I've heard that many times before and always wonder how much consideration they've given to walking.

Anyway, he had her smiling, convinced it wasn't necessarily her time to go. He glanced over a couple of minutes later and noticed the white knuckles again. He said, "What's wrong now?" She said, "Well, you know the pilot that's flying the plane?" He said, "Yes." She said, "Well, what if it's HIS time?"

Okay. I admit I'm not that fearful. However, I know there are risks and I do give some thought to them. For example, I've thought about going bungee-jumping. What's held me back from plummeting straight down and bouncing around? I don't like hanging upside down like a bat, for one thing…then, what about the bungee cord? It could be brand-new, bought that morning, but it could still be defective. I just don't have a good feeling about it. So, no bungee-jumping.

BUT, sky diving…sky diving was always at the back of my mind. That sounded like a fantastic experience. Years later, I got my chance. While out here visiting Rob again, he told me he had hosted a wine tasting and one of the men had just come from a sky dive. Everyone got excited and wanted to hear about it. He was an experienced skydiver who packed his own chute, but explained that anyone without experience could go tandem; the person you're attached to handles the whole thing. He said he could sign interested people up for the sky dive on the following Sunday. Twelve eager people signed up. Well. We have to remember that this was a WINE-tasting…by Monday, only three still wanted to go.

When Rob told me was going to see three of his friends go skydiving, I said, "O-h-h, really?" He said, "Uh, you want to go?" I said, "YEAH!" I signed up and paid up online. When asked "How many people," I was going to ask Rob if I could treat him too, when I remembered what happened on the glider ride. Lord knows WHAT might happen on a sky dive! I prudently decided not to mention it.

That Sunday Rob and I and his two little girls set out to see grandma take off. In my photo album is a copy of everything I had to sign and initial before takeoff. You'll see no less than 31 disclaimers! Here are a couple of examples:

Disclaimer Number 4: "I agree to indemnify and hold all above parties harmless from claims, judgments and costs including attorney's fees incurred in connection with any action brought as a result of my participation in parachuting activities, and in caps, including NEGLIGENCE OF THE RELEASED PARTIES, or hidden, latent, or obvious defects on the drop zone or in the equipment or aircraft used." They mentioned the dangers and risks countless times.

My favorite was Disclaimer #16 where they finally got

around to mentioning possible death. "I certify that considering my lifestyle and the manner in which I am supporting my dependants, I have made adequate provisions for my spouse, children, heirs and all other persons dependant on me so that in the event of my death they will have suffered no financial loss." I beg your pardon? What about the loss of me?

"I will not sue if, I will not sue if…" I initialed them all. We saw a video of a sky dive, and exactly what it entailed. Each of the four of us, besides our instructors, also had a video person who would take a video and stills of the whole jump.

I told Rob I had no idea of how I would feel, once it came time to jump. I said, "If I look down at the ground, then at that gaping hole in the plane, and decide maybe this isn't such a good idea, I just won't go. I'm in this for fun, NOT a nervous breakdown."

We all talked and laughed about what was ahead. I was easily old enough to be their mother. We received large plastic eyeglasses to protect our eyes as we speeded through the air. We were all going in the same plane; the pilot, four instructors, four video techs and four brand-new student skydivers. We were shown the harnesses that would connect us to the instructor. Our video techs were interviewing us all this time about our backgrounds and how we came to do this. We thought, just before the jump, that it would probably be a good idea to visit the bathroom.

I was so excited I forgot to be scared. I asked my skydiver if, as we landed, he wanted me to start running, and he said "NO!" I want you to hold your legs out as straight and high in front of you as you can. Let ME worry about the landing. He was a pretty big guy, and afterward I realized that of course he needed me to stay out of his way. If I tried to run I would just have succeeded in tangling our legs up.

We had received our instructions. Randy was the lucky one who got to jump first. Then it was my turn. My instructor said, "Are you ready?" I took a deep breath and said, "Let's do it!" We jumped out of the plane. I held onto the suspender-like straps. We had been told to keep our hands there until the instructor tapped us on the shoulder. I held on through the free fall. The free fall lasts about one minute. Our free-fall speed was, <u>minimum,</u> 120 miles per hour, depending upon our combined weight. Wow, it was FAST! I got an even bigger rush than when I went parasailing! All this time, my video tech was filming. How he managed it was beyond me. In both the video and the photos you can see the effect the "G"s are making on our cheeks.

Then the instructor pulled the string for our parachute to open. We flipped head-over-teacup, then stabilized. We were told that the instructor looks up at the parachute to be sure all is okay. Then he taps the student on the shoulder. It was so quiet. Our speed went down to about 20 miles per hour. How serene, just drifting gently. No propane noise. I waved, and blew kisses to the video camera. This lasted about five minutes. Then we hit the ground! We made a three-point landing: his knees and my nether end.

I couldn't stop grinning. My video tech had filmed our descent...how did he DO that? How did he get down before us? He asked me if I had enjoyed it and I said, "If I had done this 25 years ago, this would be my JOB right now!"

I will tell you what Randy told my son the next day (he worked for Rob). He said, "Rob, I was scared. I mean, I was really scared when we were up in that airplane. I decided I was NOT going to jump. Then I looked over at Lorraine and groaned inwardly, 'Rob's 70 year old MOTHER is going to jump!'"

He loved it though, and was glad he went. When people ask me why I do these things they consider stupid and I consider exciting, I remember a story about a man who had a flat tire. It was just outside a mental institution and a resident was inside the bars, watching as he changed it. The driver's hand slipped and all 4 lug nuts rolled down into a sewer. He was nonplussed as to what to do next. As he sat there bewildered for a moment, the resident said, "Hey, mister, just take one lug nut from the other 3 tires and put the spare on. They'll hold you until you get to a garage." The man looked up, amazed, and said, "That's great! Thanks!" He paused. "Hey, what the heck are you doing in there?" The man replied, "I'm crazy. I'm not stupid." I think I can understand that.

A Male Dummy?

A friend suggested I take a male dummy when driving cross-country. I do know one or two, actually, but no one I'd want to take on an extended trip. By the time I left upstate NY Tuesday, March 29, 1994, both the Prelude and I were on overload. Packed what I could, sent the computer set-up (timed to arrive two or three days after me) and my wonderful family would ship the rest.

My route was well planned; reservations at motels with pools where I could swim any kinks out. The longest mileage in any one day was 385. I know now I could have made it in an easy four days, but had never driven solo longer than three hours and didn't want to put any more pressure on myself than I could handle. It was traumatic enough leaving a good job, my home town in upstate New York for almost 60 years, family and friends to drive – alone – nearly 1800 miles. Why do I get the impression they're reading this, hands on hips, asking, "Then why did you GO, Lorraine?"

The Southwest had been calling to me a long time. I had written in my journal almost two years earlier, "Have felt strongly that Santa Fe is to be my next home". And, while I wasn't exactly sure whether I'd end up a best-selling author or bag lady, I knew I had to go.

I found I liked driving alone…flicking through the radio stations (no diskettes or CD's then)…stopping when/if I pleased. The first motel in Bellville Ohio was lovely. The pool in the atrium was Olympic size and I swam my 500 yards in almost complete privacy.

The clerk said a complimentary breakfast would be served in the morning. As he described it, it sounded like a full-blown brunch. Great! Who could ask for more? Uh, actually, **I** could. There was no restaurant! (Never thought to ask.) My dinner was comprised of cheese, crackers and a Kit-Kat for dessert. No way was I going out again.

Next stop, Effingham, Illinois. Another huge pool almost all to myself, and, TA-DAA! a restaurant! I had the pleasure of playing an elegant baby grand piano in the lobby for half an hour or so. I had given most of my furniture away without a second thought but still felt a pang of regret when I remembered them carrying away my "Petite Grand". Tried to swim laps in a crowded pool, but left after seven or eight "Pardons". After dinner I read about St. Louis in the travel book. Two tourist attractions listed were **The Dog Museum** and **The Bowler's Hall of Fame.** Yes. Well. I'm sure they were real big points of interest. To someone.

"O-O-O-Oklahoma, where the wind comes sweeping down the plains!" Did it ever! Wind constantly buffeted the car. When I stopped, it almost swept me into the gas station. I asked the attendant if it was unusual and he said, no, the song was right on. Back on the road, one little car very nearly changed lanes unintentionally. Kept seeing signs, "Don't Drive Into The Smoke". There wasn't any smoke, but if there had been, I'm pretty sure I would've resisted the temptation to drive into it. I couldn't understand the attraction, but evidently people there have to fight it. A lot.

The Texas Panhandle was B-O-R-I-N-G. Both the scenery and THE radio station. That's right. One. Got to Shamrock about 3:00 PM. Changed my reservation and drove another hour and a half to Amarillo. When I got there, I decided I liked staying in smaller towns. An occasional restaurant might be missing, but the swimming is great. In Amarillo the pool was crowded with beaucoup kids. I decided to give it up, have dinner, get a good night's sleep and head out early. As I prepared for bed I caught myself smiling eagerly, wondering about my apartment. I had leased it, unfurnished and sight unseen for one year. Sometimes you just have to take that leap of faith. Next stop, Santa Fe.

New Mexico's state motto is "The Land of Enchantment" and the state bird is the roadrunner. The state flower might be the yucca, but as of April 2, 1994, there was one Lorraine ROSE added to the population. I drove to the apartment complex, carried in a lamp, beach chair and sleeping bag. I sat down, took a deep breath and said aloud, "Okay, Santa Fe, I'm here. What's next?"

I carved out a nice little life for myself, writing feature stories for The New Mexican, Santa Fe's city newspaper, joining the "Que Pasa?" singles, picking up a little extra change playing piano and singing, becoming a docent in the Modern Art Museum, volunteering at the Opera Shop so I could see all the operas for free and **loving** the weather!

How in the world did that lead, three years later, to Teaching English as a Foreign Language in Warsaw Poland? Which, by the way, could rival Rochester, New York for cold winters! Hm. I see chapters about "A Rose in Poland" in my future…your future too?

From Eel Skin Shoes to Lamb Suede Bikinis

(This was my first published article in Santa Fe.)

"Can you believe those were mine," said David Gallegos as he points to a pair of tiny red cowboy boots behind glass-covered shelves. He shakes his head, smiling. His shop, Square Deal, on Johnson Street is the last place in Santa Fe where you can buy leather goods completely handmade on the premises.

Also, on the shelf with moccasins he made many years ago, are elegant eel skin shoes.

"I made these as a gift for a Hollywood movie director. He gave me quite a bit of business when Silverado was filmed in Santa Fe. He took off and I don't have an address."

Square Deal started about 90 years ago when an American Indian, who Gallegos' grandfather took in, showed his grandfather how to make moccasins and braid. He also learned to do his own tanning.

It stayed a part-time business until after World War I, when Gallegos' father started repairing and making shoes and boots full time.

"He was an orthopedic man, very good in his profession. It's too bad I didn't learn that too, because there are a lot of people with troubled feet."

Gallegos may not be an orthopedic man, but judging from the satisfied customers in and out of the shop one afternoon, he certainly knows how to mold a last (a wood or iron form) to fit each individual foot. There are 12 shelves crowded with lasts, with all different types of toes and heels.

He has more in his garage and "all over the place" in no particular order, but "I know what's there." He also stocks new lasts, but not for women's dress heels. There are just too many styles to keep them in stock.

What is the most unusual request he has gotten?

"I had a lady come in one time who asked me to make her a bikini outfit out of lamb suede. I said I'd be glad to make it for her, but I would be very embarrassed."

He cautioned her not to go in the water because the leather would be ruined if it got wet.

"She just wanted something different, you know. So

she gave me a pattern, I ordered the leather and finally did make it for her. I always make whatever the customer wants."

In shoes, the customer selects leather, color, styles, toes and heels. "They tell us what they want, and we help them. What kind of toe would be best for the foot. If an individual has callouses or bunions, I ask them what's more important - style or comfort? Ladies usually put style a little before comfort."

There are more than 20 leathers from which to choose: smooth Italian calf, rugged bull hide and exotics including kangaroo, ostrich and shark. Some, like elephant, are on the protective list. He brings out a stingray - even now a creature of grace ... and mystery.

I admire it as he confers with his workers, Isidro Robledo and Harald Jerger. None of his children or grandchildren are interested in learning the trade, but Gallegos is philosophical. "If you have to work for a living, you may as well do something you enjoy."

One-of-a-kind belts and handbags are displayed on one wall. Gallegos does his own leather carving, then dyes the belts. He has a remarkably good eye for color.

A man comes in to pick up his daughter's shoes and admires a pair of almost-finished mule skin "buckaroo boots," He jokes with us but keeps going back to the boots- a rich mahogany brown. He turns them over in his hands with appreciation, then puts them down reluctantly.

"Man, I love those boots. Love those boots!"

Gallegos says, "Well, I got your last. Just let me know if you want a pair."

I comment that the customer will be back in Square Deal soon. Where else can you custom order not only shoes, handbags, belts and boots? But also a lamb suede bikini outfit.

He laughs and then gets thoughtful.

"I sure hope she didn't go in the water with that suit on."

∞∞∞

Anxiety Attack

Hey, you know how cake mixes have special instructions for baking over 6,500 feet? Guess who follows them? Yep. Santa Fe residents, who live 7,168 feet above sea level. Well, except for me. I gave up baking for Lent years ago and it so simplified my life I never went back to it.

My apartment in Santa Fe was clean, freshly painted and LARGE. My furniture, which had taken up so much room in my car, looked pitifully skimpy here. It consisted of one low beach chair, a three-legged table that looked a bit like a large milking stool, and a small lamp. My sleeping bag and pillow did their best to fill the bedroom. Oh, and I had a few tables which the uninformed might easily mistake for cardboard boxes.

I thought I had a roommate! Exploring everything in my new home, I opened my living room double doors leading to the porch. To the right of me was another door. I was puzzled and definitely not pleased... there had been no mention of sharing – ANYTHING. Knocking first, I opened the door, walked in and almost jumped out of my skin! Heart pounding, I stared directly into a face not five inches away from mine, just as big-eyed and scared. No wonder. It was me. I was looking into my full-length mirrored bedroom closet. Yes. Well. I do lead an interesting life.

A friend who spent winters here in New Mexico and summers back east lived in the next apartment complex. She stopped by and asked if I'd like to go to a senior low-impact aerobics class with her the next day. Not wanting to be rude, I accepted. When she left, I smiled to myself. I may have been pushing 60, but six days a week I either jogged three miles or swam 800 yards. Senior aerobics? Piece of cake.

We got there and I easily began following the steps of the director. Half way through I found myself breathing harder and feeling fatigued. I never had an anxiety attack but by the time we finished, I felt like this was a full-blown one. My heart was beating, I couldn't fill my lungs and I was exhausted. I talked to the director, wondering if I should check in with a doctor. Oh, right, I didn't have one yet. She asked where I was from, and when I told her I had lived in Upstate New York all my life, she said, "Sea level, right?" I nodded. "When did you get here?" When I told her I had driven in yesterday, she shook her head, unbelievingly. "From zero to 7,000 feet in what? Four or five days? Don't you know how thin the air is at this altitude? Don't you realize how dry it is? How low the humidity is?" I shook my head, abashed, like a schoolgirl who hadn't done her homework and was being given a pop quiz. "Your BODY is having an anxiety attack! It's wondering where all the oxygen is! Now", speaking more gently, "You have to drink, drink, drink plenty of water, even if you're not thirsty, and exercise **gradually.** Take short walks. Slow down in class…stop often… breathe…listen to your body." I nodded, penitently.

My friend offered to loan me her bed, card table and futon. It would save her storage space and give me time to look for my own. Of course, I had to wait a month until she left. FINALLY I had a bed on which to lay down my weary head. It had been very weary at times, between the altitude and aerobics five times a week. I got a huge kick out of exercising with a former movie star, though. (Those too young to remember Tab Hunter are to be pitied.)

There were more challenges. My hair, always, so manageable with its gentle body perm, went wild! I was complaining to a friend and she asked if I was finally going grey. Grey? No! Grey I could have handled. My lovely hair had turned into something like steel wool. How could it be kind of kinky and yet stick straight out at the same time? It responded to **nothing**. I applied enough conditioners to cause softening of the brain. The hairdresser explained that my hair was in culture shock. Yeah, well so was **I** every time I looked in the mirror. I had an overwhelming urge to call out, "ha-ha-ha-HA-ha! I didn't know whether to fly off with Woody Woodpecker, or get a buzz. Both kinds.

The culture shock continued in other ways. The Santa Fe Reporter headline (regarding the gubernatorial election) actually read, "Does it matter who's governor?"

Bumper stickers about alcohol weren't new, but these were worded a tad differently: "Don't drink and drive… you might spill your drink." I grinned when I went by the "Yippy-I-Aye" Trading Co., and really got a kick out of the phone company. After she got all the information to install my new land line (no cell phones then) a cheerful US West employee rang off with an enthusiastic, "All righty-roonie!"

I nodded, smiling to myself and thought, Yep, I think I'm going to like it here.

An Axe Murderer

Okay. January 2012. A friend said, "If you want to meet someone who's as active as you, someone to go dancing with, then write to an organization that matches people up." So, I did. They sent me tons of matches. Not tons of good matches, you understand. Hey, it ain't easy when you're slightly past the three-quarter century mark, no matter HOW healthy you are.

I heard from two men right off the bat. Both in their fifties. Yeah, I'm pretty sure they wanted mommy to take care of them. (Ya think?) When I first moved to Florida…. Uh, did I mention I was now living in Venice, Florida? Come on, keep up, people. Anyway, a new acquaintance (a new, sarcastic, skeptical acquaintance) had told me that in her experience, men were looking for either a nurse or a purse. I met with one man who had a nice bio, and a nice smile. We had coffee and said goodbye…nicely.

So. I read another bio…a guy who hunted, fished, camped and traveled with a 5th wheel. I only knew about a 3rd wheel (extra person on a date). He was nothing like what I was looking for. He did, however, have a great sense of humor. This, and the fact that we both love to travel were about all we had in common. His on-line name was "Angler" and mine was "Zingara" (Italian for "Gypsy").

He said he'd go to whatever lengths he had to, to find the right woman to travel with. Said he actually drove from Indiana down to Texas to meet a woman. Yep. Actually drove right back the next day. I was still laughing when I wrote that while I liked his sense of humor and we both loved travel, we definitely were NOT a match.

I explained that the last time I fished was when I was four, with my dad. He set up our poles, said to be quiet, and if my pole moved, it meant I had a fish. Yes. Well. I waited. And waited. And WAITED. Hey, it may have only been half an hour, but to a four-year old, being quiet and sitting still that long is two days, easy. I decided I had waited long enough. Example of four-year old logic: If the pole moves, it means I have a fish. Ergo, the pole must move. (Ergo. Pretty good vocab for a 4-year old, eh?)

When daddy looked the other way, I gave it a nudge. A really, really big one. It started moving wildly; he picked it up and found only a sad little half-drowned worm. Shades of Jose Cuervo. He gave me a look – we all know that look, right? "Snippy?" Now. I want you to know that nickname was no reflection on my personality. When I was born he said I was a little snippet of a thing, and I was his "Snippy" from then on. "Did you kick that pole?" "Yes daddy." "Don't do it again." "No daddy."

Well, "Angler" appreciated MY humor, and suggested we meet. "Angler" and "Zingara" became Jimmy and Lorraine.

∞∞∞

We lunched on a Florida beach one breezy, sunny day, drank the ice wine he brought, and talked the whole afternoon. He was a very easy man to be with. The hours passed with us chatting; laughing comfortably together. I didn't say it, but found myself thinking how pleasant it would be to watch the sunset together. He had traveled all around the USA to various places, but the biggest trip was to Canada for three months every year to fish, and get out of the hot Florida summers. Hm. Fishing. What a treat.

He showed me pictures from the fishing resort in Canada. The scenery, which was lovely, friends getting together, the boats in the lake, a bear breaking into garbage someone had forgotten to cover…a bear…A BEAR!! He said, hoping to reassure me, "It was only a cub." "Jimmy," I said earnestly, "They have parents!"

Then he asked me if I could bake a blueberry pie. I was surprised because we weren't talking about food at all. The question seemed to just come out of the blue (so to speak). I said I'd baked many pies over the years, although maybe not blueberry. It seems he has a cache of frozen wild Canadian blueberries which he had picked, and LOVED blueberry pies, pancakes, etc. I nodded, noncommittally.

We talked of snags, hurdles and obstacles (all on my part) which would prevent my going to Canada with him. He suggested that maybe if I saw his 5th wheel, it might sway my thinking. I was pretty sure which way my thinking would sway, but agreed to see it. The next day he would pick me up and drive us to Bradenton, about an hour away.

When my friend Marla told her husband that I went off for the day with a guy I only met the day before he was shocked and worried. "She doesn't even KNOW him! He could be an axe murderer!" Actually, I amazed myself with my decision. Usually I'm a fairly cautious person. The only reason I can give is that I felt comfortable with him…safe, even. It didn't occur to me until much later that probably the axe murderer's victims felt that exact same way. Oh, well.

Okay. The 5th Wheel. He explained that the camper is 34 feet long with two sliders. The only sliders I had ever heard of wore baseball uniforms. Oh yeah, and those little tiny hamburgers. I learned that two sides of the camper actually slid out to the side enlarging the living space considerably. Granted, the 5th wheel was a generous size, but there would still be a lot of, uh, togetherness. In the truck, side by side. In the 5th wheel, mm-hm. Yep…24/7…close.

Our differences looked to be insurmountable. Snags, hurdles and obstacles! (Oh, my.) Besides his huge black truck and camper he owned a good-sized fishing boat, 2 smaller boats, a scooter and a Harley Davidson. Oh, and a quad. Here we go again. I learned that a quad is NOT one quarter of quadruplets, it's an ATV. Which is…? An All-Terrain-Vehicle. Oh. One of those things with the big balloon-y wheels.

This guy has toys! AND, he's a real outdoor man. Camper, fisherman, biker, hunter (now only with a camera, but still…) and me? A small town girl who lived in the same town she was born in for 59 years. Writer, musician, taught English as a Foreign Language in Europe for three years. I never fished or hunted, never camped out, never was in the Girl Scouts, never even learned to pee outside, for gosh sakes!

I told Marla that although he and I had a lot in common, I thought he was a really nice guy and I hoped he'd find a match. She suggested introducing him to her friend Sally, who was a real outdoor person…had bred horses and dogs, had lived on a farm, had actually lived in a 5th wheel for a year, and was interested in meeting someone compatible. Bingo!

I emailed him the next day and said he'd given me a lot to think about, and I'd be calling him. After a day or so I called and said, basically, that he was a nice guy, but I wasn't the outdoor type; fishing, bears and wilderness is not my thing, etc. However, I knew a woman who might be interested. Would he like to meet her? Of course! Sally was a tad apprehensive, but said she'd go. When she didn't call him for a couple of days, he called me and said he hadn't heard from her, and if she was nervous about meeting him alone, he'd take us both to lunch. I left a message on her phone.

Sally called him, a lunch date was set. Then she called me and asked if I'd go…she'd feel better with me along. Sure. We had a really pleasant time. He mentioned the blueberry pie to her. We both kidded him about the song, "Billy Boy" – Can she bake a cherry pie, Billy Boy, Billy Boy….and we all laughed. We got back to her house and she asked us both in. He grinned and said, "No, I know you just want to talk about me." After he drove off I asked her expectantly, "Well? What do you think?" She retorted, "What do I think? What do I think, Lorraine? I think he likes YOU!"

But that wasn't her only problem. Seems she was **REALLY** apprehensive about all this. Had I heard about that man who had killed so many women that he had met online? And so on. Said she might consider going out with Jimmy again, but I thought it didn't seem likely. Well, I had tried.

After a couple of days, Jimmy called me to ask if I knew whether or not she was going to call. I said I didn't know, I just delivered the messages and he shouldn't shoot the messenger. He called back about twenty minutes later and said that while he wasn't surprised that I didn't want to go to Canada, he really liked my company, and would I like to go out to lunch once in a while?

I said, "Of course, we could be friends. I'd like that."

I hung up the phone, smiling.

Email, References and Reasons Not to Go--

MANY REASONS NOT TO GO....

Jimmy and I saw each other occasionally. So far he hadn't met anyone else.

Emails...

Hey Jimmy. I've been thinking about your dilemma and wrote new words to "Billy Boy" to cheer you up. They're attached. Hope you like them. Lorraine.
P.S. *If you can't bring them in, let me know.*

Well, good evening Lorraine. I just want you to know that I am too dumb when it comes to these computers because I see that you did send something called Billy Boy but if you want me to hear what you composed you will have to either sing it over the phone or meet me somewhere because that's the only way I'll ever hear it. Jimmy

Okay. Maybe I'll call sometime or sing it when I see you. This will give me a chance to write that last verse. I'll make you a copy, too. How's the search going? Can I be nosy and ask if Sally called back? Has anyone else responded? Find anyone to bake that Blueberry Pie? Lorraine

Well good morning, Lorraine. I just opened my email and see that you have a few questions. The search is currently going nowhere. Sally has not responded by phone or carrier pigeon so I do not expect to hear from her at all. Jimmy

P.S. *No one has baked me a blueberry pie!*

That three-month Canada trip is a bit of a hurdle, isn't it? Maybe you should try short trips first. I'm curious as to how it all works. Do each others' habits (singing, reading signs aloud, snapping gum) drive both of you a little crazy? I could make up a story filled with comical situations. Good luck. Lorraine

Would you consider taking a short trip with me? That could be arranged. In the meantime you can write that last verse to Billy Boy. By the way did I tell you I come with excellent references? I can give you the name and phone number of someone I traveled with for almost two years. She's happily married now, but we parted friends. Jimmy

Now, I'm not promising anything, but I'm thinking about the difference between baking a pie using domestic blueberries and wild ones. JUST THINKING. I'm sure you have to use more berries because they're smaller. What about sugar? Are they sweeter? I was telling my friend Marla about it, and said it would be just my luck to have it turn out runny. She said, "No problem. Just serve it with ice cream and tell him it's a Blueberry Cobbler." I could do that. I once scorched the vanilla pudding and told my husband it was caramel. He bought it. Hm. Well, I'll finish my glass of wine (not ice wine) and say goodnight. Lorraine

Well good morning to you, Lorraine. I am just sitting in my camper and wondering how you are doing and trying to think of what there is to do. How would you like to take a drive with me to Tarpon Springs this coming Saturday? You can sing the blueberry pie song on the way. Hope you will have time to respond. --Jimmy

Thanks, but Saturday – in fact this whole week—is impossible. I've never been to Tarpon Springs. It's pretty far, right? I'm committed to getting ready for and working on my church's yard sale. Sorting things Thursday and Friday and working the sale on Saturday. I'll probably make a couple of cakes too. (Whew! Maybe I should be committed.) Just kidding. I like doing it or I wouldn't have volunteered. Thanks again for the invite. --Lorraine

Okay, then, when????????????????????? Jimmy

NOTE: We spent the following Saturday at Tarpon Springs. We had a lovely day. His behavior was considerate, respectful and gentlemanly...asked if he could hold my hand. We had a delicious fish lunch, walked around the town, bought sponges, he bought a loofa for his daughter, went to the little museum and watched a video. (There wasn't an axe in sight.) He said he was going to leave February 13 to spend one week in the Everglades and two weeks in the Keys. Would I think about going with him?

Emails again, still January...

Hey, Jimmy! Sleep was eluding me (are we surprised?) So much to think about. Had a glass of wine to relax me. It didn't. The only thing I know about the Florida Everglades is that it's a swamp. As long as I was awake I decided to look it up on the computer. Uh-oh. Mistake. BIG mistake. Huge! mosquitos, crocodiles, alligators (BOTH?), Florida panthers (PANTHERS?), mosquitos... I mention mosquitos twice because they have the biggest vote, by a landslide. Nothing I read reassured me (again, are we surprised?) It's going on 1:30AM and my eyes are still very wide open. Below are a few comments: Countless birds, deer, raccoons, multitude of mosquito bites, manatees, bald eagles, bugs seem immune to repellent so wear long pants and cover your arms...no, No, NO! I can't picture me there. Sorry. -- Lorraine

NOTE: I talked with my firstborn, whose words <u>always</u> come from a good place, and when she said, "Let's talk about this...JIMMY. I braced myself for what would come next. Wow, I was completely caught off guard with her next words: "You know, mom, when you talk about Jimmy, I hear something in your voice that I haven't heard in a long, long time. There's a softness in your tone."

We talked some more, and after last Sunday's sermon from Rev. Patricia which covered being open, praying for guidance, taking a chance, listening to your heart and the God within, writing that book you've been putting off for years, meditating and trusting your decisions (were there any of my buttons she had missed?)

I decided to make that "character reference" phone call. She confirmed all the "gut feelings" I had about Jimmy. She said, "He's a gentle, generous considerate GOOD man." They had always gotten along well…the breakup had to do with conflict between her and his family. She didn't elaborate and I didn't ask.

Jimmy called to ask if I had made up my mind about the Everglades. He hadn't read my fearful message yet. I read him all the scary information. He said he didn't really want to influence me, but he thought much of it had been exaggerated. "There aren't any more mosquitos in the everglades than in Canada!" I said, "And this is supposed to reassure me?" We set a date to talk some more.

Emails: February, 2012…

Good morning, Jimmy. What are your exact dates for the Everglades and Keys? Lorraine

Good morning to you right back. Now a simple phone call would have been simpler but here goes. I will leave Bradenton on the 12th for the Everglades. I'll get to Marathon Key on the 19th and stay until March 4th. I think I have a way to keep you happy and keep me out of the DOG HOUSE. We will get into that Tuesday. Jimmy

Didn't you say you'd leave Bradenton a day later if you had a passenger? One that didn't take up too much room?

P.S., I love it when anyone wants to keep me happy. L

NOTE: Jimmy called to say we could leave on the 13th and that he had a few ideas to discuss on Tuesday. "We're still on, right?" I said yes. I also told him I had checked his "character references". I repeated what I'd said before; it often looks like I make snap decisions, but I research every decision well, even if it involves staying up half the night for two, three or **many** nights. I usually go with my gut feeling.

He said if he went with his gut feelings, he'd probably get his face slapped. I burst out laughing—he did too, and we agreed it's a great way to start out the day. I asked if he played Scrabble, cards, Chinese Checkers? Nope. He hadn't played cards in years and that was only Black Jack and Poker. And Chinese Checkers **longer** ago. I said, "I guess Scrabble is out, too. (Sigh.) My daughter Audrey would say, 'Mother, get a ladder and get over it!' So I will. Fortunately, these answers weren't dealbreakers. Well, goodbye for now. I have to go find my ladder." We laughed.

Yes, I went with him. We laughed a lot, and enjoyed getting to know each other better. We stayed OUTSIDE the Everglades, but toured it. It had been unusually dry so mosquitos weren't a big problem. (Jimmy wanted to take credit for that.) I **did** enjoy the Keys.

Jimmy said, coaxingly, when he brought me back home, "I bet you'd enjoy the Canadian trip, too." I looked at him doubtfully, and answered truthfully, "Jimmy, I don't think so. Fishing? In the Arctic Watershed? Closest grocery 50 miles away? For three months? I can't even believe I'm considering it." He said, "You'll love it, wait and see."

He sounded so sure, but I didn't know. I wasn't sure I had enough ladders.

Billy Boy

OH WHERE HAVE YOU BEEN, JIMMY BOY?

(Parody by Lorraine Rose)

∞∞∞

Oh, where have you been, Jimmy Boy, Jimmy Boy,
Oh, where have you been, charming Jimmy?
To Bay Indies once again, all the way from Bradenton,
Hoped a lady would share my truck and 5th wheel.

Will you go to Canada, Jimmy Boy, Jimmy Boy
Will you go to Canada, charming Jimmy?
I will go to Canada, even drive to Shangri-la,
If that lady will share my truck and 5th wheel.

Did you get your berry pie, Jimmy Boy, Jimmy Boy,
Did you get your berry pie, charming Jimmy?
Wild blueberries I have got, but the pie I still have not,
And no lady to share my truck and 5th wheel.

Oh, what will you do Jimmy Boy, Jimmy Boy,
Oh what will you do, charming Jimmy?
I'm so blue that I could cry, like the berries for that pie,
Where's that lady to share my truck and 5th wheel?

Are your hopes still so high, Jimmy Boy, Jimmy Boy,

Are your hopes still so high, charming Jimmy?
High as mountains in the sky,
I've been promised me a pie,
Surely someone will share my truck and 5th wheel.

Bobcats and Shoplifting

Jimmy spent every June, July and August fishing in Canada. And he wanted me to leave Florida and live in Canada (you notice I say "live" - not "vacation") for three months? Well, tep months, actually; every summer I spend a month back east with my family. Still. Two months. At a fishing resort. Um...fishing. In Canada. Yeah, I'm pretty sure it would take me all of three days to change the spelling of "fishing" to "b-o-o-o-o-o-o-ring!" And how long have you known this guy, Lorraine?

Besides, I was finally getting used to living in Florida, and believe me, it wasn't always easy. Three years before, I had arrived in August, and it was the first time I experienced a 98 degree temperature with 100% humidity! My skin was the only part of me that was happy. Talk about your moisturizer!

I was in Venice, Florida, in a 55 plus (and let me tell you, there were a lot of very "plus" residents) mobile home complex. To be fair, a lot of lively residents lived there, too. There was a three-mile path around the complex and I tried to walk it almost every day. In order to beat the summer heat I walked just before the sun rose, or much later, after sundown. The park manager was horrified when she found out. She said never to go on the path alone that early or that late…I might encounter a bobcat. WHAT? She said they didn't bother people, as a rule, but if a person happened to startle one…. Yep, she didn't have to tell me twice. I'd get my daily exercise in one of the three pools. Better get another swimsuit.

Wouldn't you think the summer wear would be really reasonable? Some was, of course, but the bathing suits I liked were quite pricey. Not to worry. I had become proficient at getting discounts, even when they weren't offered. Take note, people: I went to the counter with my choice, and said to the salesgirl, "Of course, you give senior discounts." She said, uncertainly, "Uh, no, I don't think so." Well, YOU can't see my lower lip start to quiver, but SHE sure could. Afraid she was going to have a sobbing old lady on her hands, she said quickly, "Wait. I'll ask the manager." I couldn't hear the words spoken, but I could hear his tone (grumbling) and hers (pleading). His voice kept getting louder and finally I heard him say clearly (and angrily), "Oh, all right, give her $5.00 off." YESSSS!!! It worked again! I wasn't surprised. I had perfected that lower lip quiver years ago. It actually got me out of getting a ticket for going the wrong way on a one way street!

I was laughing about this with one of my grandsons, and said, "Zack, I bet I could use that to my advantage in other ways. Maybe shoplifting? He started to say cautiously, "Uh, gram, I don't think…." I said, "Now, just hear me out. If I steal the article and DON"T get caught, I've got it, right?" He said, a little alarmed, "Gram, you're not really...." I interrupted him. "BUT, if I do get caught, I could always do the lip quiver, right?" He said nervously, "Gram, now you're scaring me!"

No, of course I would never do it, but I didn't tell my family that. I kept mentioning shoplifting, kiddingly, but they were never quite sure of me. Good! Keep them all a bit on edge. They can get too complaisant, always thinking of grandma in the kitchen baking cookies or taking the grandchildren to the movies. (Two things, by the way, I DO enjoy.) Now, pictures of grandma in handcuffs were creeping into their thoughts. I bet they'd be so relieved when it didn't happen, they would be much more understanding if I took off and taught in Europe for three years, or much less worried if I decided to travel around the country with a gentleman, sans wedding bells. I could almost hear them thinking, "Well, at least she's not in jail." Yep, I could feel this working for me.

But was I ready to leave Florida and do that? Who would sing "Old Time Rock and Roll" at Karaoke on Friday nights? I would miss performing in the yearly show we put on. One year I even had the fun of directing it. On the other hand...I do love to travel. But how about those Saturday dances at the Moose Club? Yeah, and I was getting really good at clogging and line dancing. But on the other hand...uh, I think I just ran out of hands.

LORRAINE ROSE

∞∞∞

Lorraine Rose:

Author Profile

L orraine Rose led a conventional life as wife, mother and grandmother for many years. Read how this changed dramatically in her late 40's. She received a B.A. in college and began freelance writing. which included a column for a Women's magazine. Her column covered the problems, perils and (often comical) challenges of being, "On My Own Again."

Almost 60 then, she drove, alone, 1800 miles from her home in upstate New York to rent an apartment, sight unseen, in Santa Fe, New Mexico, where she wrote feature stories for the city newspaper, *The New Mexican.*

Travel with her as she parasails, goes up in balloons and gliders and once even jumped out of a perfectly good airplane. She taught English in Warsaw, Poland, for three years, although she isn't Polish and wasn't a teacher (the topic of her next book coming soon). Her adventures also included traveling around the United States, Canada and Mexico in a 5th wheel for a few years.

In her eighties now, she lives (in her words, "For how long?") in San Diego, California, where she continues her writing.

The Manor Publishing Collective

The Manor Publishing Collective (MPC), founded by Sunny J. Baker, Ph.D., is a unique venture of former authors and would-be authors who want to share their ideas, experiences and creativity with the world—but who don't necessarily want to learn the technologies of the 21st Century to make it happen. Dr. Baker's background in computers and experience writing 28 books with traditional publishers, fueled the idea while having lunch with the talented residents at St. Paul's Manor in San Diego. Dr. Baker produces the books, designs the covers and completes the social marketing aspects for the books and MPC. The other members of the collective simply write and create!

The first members of MPC all live at St. Paul's Manor, an independent seniors' community. Currently, the average age of the 120 residents is 82 years of productive living. The oldest member of the MPC today is Glenn Flenniken, 95, who is still writing experiential poetry like crazy. His first volume is already in production and his second volume is already in progress. If you enjoy his wit and romantic take on life, please look for his works on Kindle at Amazon.com! We think you'll enjoy

Lorraine Rose's stories just as well--full of true life adventure, humor and insights! She also has two more volumes in the production queue already. You're sure to enjoy them all!

For your information, the royalties shared by the collective authors will be exactly that—shared by all members of the collective and also shared with the residents' association at St. Paul's Manor, housed in a sixty-year-old building that sorely needs upgrades, more activities for residents and other enhancements to make the remaining years of life even more vigorous and rewarding. Please support these incredible seniors and their community by looking for all the new publications by MPC authors.

Books In This Series

Manor Publishing Collective -- First Titles

MPC calls these "books by seniors online." All of these books are written by members of the Manor Publishing Collective (MPC). You must be over 65 to participate in MPC, but you don't necessarily need to learn the technologies to get published online. MPC does that for the members of the collective. Portions of the royalties are shared among all the MPC authors.

My Early Years: The First Sixty Of So....

By Glenn Flenniken, 96 years young and still writing narrative poetry as this is being written. As one of the last surviving sailors from WWII his narrative, his descriptive poems, are gems.

Mission Possible! Social Justice And Slavery On Planet Nork...

By Leonard Sussmann, 77, an new MPC author with a viewpoint and a (science fiction) story. An egalitarian who supports Bernie Sanders' ideal, this book is a good, fun read for anyone who enjoys fictionalized history (and stories about space travel).

Hey! You Never Know... Witty Vignettes Of Life, Adventure And Insight

Lorraine Rose's first book in a series of three memoirs, full of wit, adventure and insights about life in general.

A Few Favorite Jokes...The Mostly Clean Ones

Bill Starr is already an accomplished Amazon writer, but this little book is just that--a few fun jokes from a very funny senior who is enjoying life in San Diego and who happily joined MPC to share some of his wit.

Made in the USA
Middletown, DE
09 April 2020